YOKUM
JOURNEY

ROBERT AUGUSTIN
REGNIER

authorHOUSE®

AuthorHouse™
1663 Liberty Drive
Bloomington, IN 47403
www.authorhouse.com
Phone: 1-800-839-8640

Published by AuthorHouse   08/31/2015

ISBN: 978-1-4969-0212-2 (sc)
ISBN: 978-1-5049-4748-0 (e)

Library of Congress Control Number: 2014906054

Print information available on the last page.

Any people depicted in stock imagery provided by Thinkstock are models, and such images are being used for illustrative purposes only. Certain stock imagery © Thinkstock.

This book is printed on acid-free paper.

Because of the dynamic nature of the Internet, any web addresses or links contained in this book may have changed since publication and may no longer be valid. The views expressed in this work are solely those of the author and do not necessarily reflect the views of the publisher, and the publisher hereby disclaims any responsibility for them.

KIDS LIKE TO LAUGH

Take three steps in the sand
Start a journey across the land
Who are you really, all said and done
A certain day, a certain one
Red balloon puts a smile on my face
Trouble and heartache gone without a trace
You're much too nice, our pilot of spin
Looking for a ray of light, man of tin
You can see it in shades of blue
Art in our vision for me and you
Light knows where the dreams chase
Darkest grey, satin and lace
So take me back to places near
Indian ways where we all shed a tear

OLD SCHOOL DREAMING

Sleep on a soft pillow

And dream the night away

Lean against a summer breeze

A wind that blows on a sunny day

Gravity is a hunk of wood

Showing what you learn

Precious angels give that look

Light and fast let the candle burn

Classic song, I'm ready to rock

Take me back to happy days

Counting memories one by one

Old school dreaming will change my ways

Picture the way forward

Emotion is an image
Pictures tell a tale
Creative is in its own class
Live a life we all know well
Eye catching is the sound
The art we do is worth a look
Go to school and find an answer
In the pages of an open book
A window sees an open door
An eagle shows the way
Togetherness is the song we sing
In the morning of a sunny day

WRITE ON ROCKS

Who will stir the soup

Who will satisfy the hunger within

Teaching a passion that was left behind

Abstract is a place where we all win

Stars grace a field of blue

Desire is inside our soul

Death is part of the unknown

Everywhere is a world that's whole

I will dance the night away

And sing until the wolves cry out

Only the future, only the present

Thank you Beatles for "Twist and Shout"

Robert Augustin Regnier

SITTING AROUND THE TABLE

The believer walked alone

On a lonely street lit by a bright light

I followed him down to the end

Where a little bit of everything filled the night

The whole world is watching

So let me enjoy this summer with you

The music will pull us in

Riding the sound is nothing new

The answer is waiting

Summer romance for you and me

Yes I hear our song

Flow through the boughs of an oak tree

Shadows in the Sky

The flowers are gone
Kiss tomorrow goodbye
Gone for another year
Try not to cry
But they were pretty
Brightening up my day
The flowers were my friends
Together in a special way
But thanks to good fortune
I can see shadows in the sky
Hear echoes in the wind
And live the good life never wondering why

DARK HORSE

Dark horse
Who would have thought
That talent is something
Fate would have brought
Hiding in the shadows
Lost in the weeds
Men and women toil
And do good deeds
Walking through the front door
Of life's open book
The party has just begun
So let's dance and take a look

THE WHOLE WORLD WATCHES

Love was a one way street

When I was feeling lonely and blue

But my friends where important

And God was there too

Days went bye

And magic filled the air

Time went by fast

With visions of seeing things where

Dreams were everyone's song

And lovers danced in the moon light

My heart would skip a beat

When signs of passion were in sight

I want to be with you

My special friend

I always want to see you smile

And sing with you to the end

SONG AND PLEASURE

Because of all this heartache and pain
I'll do my crying in the rain
But when birds fly in skies of blue
Joy will come to me and you
The songs we write are here to stay
Brightening our world in a spiritual way
So love is here and thank God it's true
Song and pleasure for me and you

JOHNNY ROCKET

I reached for something

The thrill of winning

The sight of wheels spinning

Or a little less sinning

But I'm barely hanging on

To a wagon ride

Where simple things hide

To where things are better on the other side

I didn't come here to start a fight

But if I have to I will

Seeing shadows in the evening light

Leads to ripples on a morning still

Robert Augustin Regnier

SUMMER GIRL

Summer girl

Looks into your eyes

And through your soul

Where our vision tells no lies

Summer time love

Will grow into more

A life time of happiness

Is what we have in store

So ride our bikes

And paddle our canoe

Run in the sun

And live our lives anew

GIRL WITH A RED DRESS

Cowboys and cowgirls
Listen to songs and watch us dance
So come a little closer my love
And we will ride the wings of romance
The bright lights of the street
Shine down on you and me
The beating of the summer sun
Gives life to the apple tree
So girl I don't care
If you call me a bad name
The world will still spin
And I'll love you just the same

VISION FROM THE OTHER SIDE

I got a melody in my head
And it will not go away
It's a song that tells the truth
So I guess it's here to stay
Treat a woman like a lady
Young girls deserve it too
Pretty girls and angels with grace
Worship in skies of blue
Find the words to say
In sentences that tell
Of poets looking back
To ripples in the wishing well
Take me down to forever
A place where my thoughts can ride
On a white horse with a silver saddle
A vision seen from the other side

TRYING TO FIND THE WAY

Bridges in time

Cover ground

Lines in the sand

Are there to be found

By the one who sits

In the rocking chair of swing town

Where pictures of people

Swirl around and around

Sailors come back

For the prizes we won

An image opens the door

And gives us love where there was none

A hundred more pages

Are here to tell

The story of exciting dreams

That look through the wishing well

Robert Augustin Regnier

POEMS FOR HER

I write poems for her
For her pretty smile
That shines down closely
With her elegant style
So knock, and the door will open
To songs that always rhyme
With gifts that always bring
A sense of togetherness, with love all the time
So give it all you got
And see the joy it will bring
Here is a toast to what it is all about
Poems for her with rhymes we softly sing

SO TIRED SO HELP US

I came down from mountain meadow

With many ways to sing

The melodies I heard under the stars

Storms with thunder and other things

So darling hear my prayer

I said it so that we can see

Emotion when it fails

To come close to us Honey Bee

Looking for an echo

In the colors of a rainbow

Staying very close

To the distant fire all of us know

The young woman runs away

From a song that breaks her heart

But by the end of the day, love will win out

So write the lyrics, and we'll never part

THE MYSTERY OF IT ALL

When the wind blows the clouds along
It makes me think of a summer song
Branches wave with leaves of green
Apples in the summer are here to be seen
Water flows from a cold spring
Echoes rolling softly is the song we sing
I write these things in a country song
A place where we gather, where our love is strong
So take the mystery out of saying goodbye
And feel the beauty of never wondering why

Soft voices

I wrote a chapter

To the one who got away

Smiling is the one who remembered

The actor who came another day

She doesn't have an easy life

A whisper or a gentle touch

But everything will turn out right

Because our sister didn't love a man to much

You might be the one who looked my way

The one who seemed so right

Dancing in the days of youth

Where soft voices grace the night

STARLIGHT BRIGHT

I fell into a whirlpool

A whirlpool of struggle

Love the sound, love world peace

And love the boy in the bubble

Diamonds in the ground

Are there for a happy soul

Take me down to ghost town

Where spirits live in the blackness of coal

Horns blow in rhyme

They carry a pleasant beat

U- la – la the young girl sings

In harmony where native sounds meet

See the image in our camera

Go to the brightest light

We see the city from the nighttime sky

Shining through a starlight bright

THIS MAGICAL LAND

The girl skips a rope

And sings a song

Baby baby, love in a trance

Where the past is never wrong

Kick a ball in the field

Play circles in the sand

Keep our memories alive

In this magical land

I remember this well

The times we strolled, me and you

So make this dance a trip back in time

These melodies that make our day so true

Robert Augustin Regnier

DRAGONS, CAROUSELS, AND TREES

Dream up lines
To tell to the beginner
Of the gallery west
Where empty chairs wait for the seer
Eyes for the lonely to see
Vision for the skyward look
Ducks in a row show the way
To learn a song from an open book
Dragons, carousels, and trees
Waiting for the show to start
Wood in place points to the stars
Black fish shows a love that will never part

TIN ROOF

A lot of things go running through my mind

When a tin roof gets to talking

Sounds of nature are here for us

When you and I go walking

Step by step the journey starts

Down the road we go

Flowers guide us along the way

The path to good times is everything we know

So throw a horse shoe for luck

And watch it fall in place

Gone is our desire for want

Negative things, gone without a trace

SYMBOLIC JOURNEY

Create the word

And cast yourself off the hill

A person who can pray

Gives us freedom and a strong will

Surrender I will

To a power within

Freedom to endure

The battles that let us win

Please don't burn the book

Let us say what we say

The message is worth a look

The revelation will come another day

Nobody can compete

With a heart so true

Last tango in paradise

Defines love for me and you

THE SONG OF A CONDOR'S WINGS

I walk down a dirt road

But there's something missing

She sings a country song

And I just try to listen

Town to town is where we look

And we find you in a place of many things

Call me a name that rhymes

With the song coming from a condor's wings

Riding up and down the trail

Gives me a taste of a country night

Even on a quiet day

We can ride the sunbeam of the morning light

Robert Augustin Regnier

COUNTRY MELODIES

Hold on and understand

The words that we write

And read them in the moment

Where we keep good loving in sight

Somebody will win

And many others will lose

I want to follow you to the end

Where I walk and where I find the clues

Light a candle

And it will take me higher

You should be dancing

Life on a wire

Celebrate the memory

In a song so true

Make it strong and make it last

Country melodies for me and you

THE MYSTERIOUS COWBOY

The mysterious cowboy rides alone

On his horse across the land

Shot gun at the ready

Six gun at hand

Indians step back

And let him ride on through

Cactus and stage brush

Sand and rocks under a sky of blue

The mysterious cowboy knows where he's going

There will only be a happy tear

Fighting for the hand of the gifted one

The mysterious cowboy has no fear

Traveling on the trail to Mexico

A bad man gets in the way

Bang bang they shoot it out

The mysterious cowboy lives another day

✳ *Robert Augustin Regnier*

HOT AIR BALLOONS

We watched the balloons rise into the sky

Colors were bright as they sailed away

The fliers were bold and daring

Destined to fly through night and day

Conditions of wind

Powered by fire

Lifts each balloon

Higher and higher

Up up they go

One by one into the night

The wind takes them on a journey

Up up and away on their intrepid flight

What a way to end a summer night

Taking pictures of colors so bright

Everybody seemed to have a good time

Ending the night with song and rhyme

GO FORWARD TOGETHER

I lived by a river

The water flowed on bye

Keep your eye on the fishing pole

Hold on to our vision of the blue sky

We got to find a way to a peace

A peace that never wonders why

I do believe that some day

We will find a way never to cry

Consider a life with no song to sing

With no poems to rhyme

Just our savior to praise

Marching in step to freedom time

Tell me more about the good

About the boys who went over the hill

Free at last says the old farmer

Singing for freedom is always a thrill

Robert Augustin Regnier

BUILT BY SWEAT AND TEARS

Let's take it easy

Let's take it slow

Mountains to climb, valleys to cross

This journey will make our love grow

Beautiful beautiful

Was the dogwood flowers

Rain made the sun

Shine for hours and hours

Outside is a gathering

Of we shall overcome

The sight of you and me walking

The march is what we have become

So we are here to tell

The truth about our golden age

The plan is to see it through

The hurdles crossed, so let's turn a page

BLACK ON WHITE

I'm going to see my girl
I'm going to dance and sing a song
Play my guitar and watch the sun come up
Melodies and vibrations are ever so strong
Come back to me Nancy Sunshine
Walk me down to the easy chair
I'm a lonely soul waiting to be touched
Sitting in the corner where I quietly stare
Sing to the back of the room
Dance in the shining light
Tell my story to the waiting fan
Dream in colors, black on white

KEEP ON SMILING

I like your eyes, so soft and brown

A smile so bright, look at what I've found

A body kissed by the sun

A lady always ready for fun

You and I go walking

Side by side

Hand and hand

So let's give our love a ride

Never slow down

Always do it right

Keep our eyes straight ahead

And keep our love in sight

THE LIFE OF THE SHEEP EATER

The result is music
And the gift is ours
Up above the clouds
Are a thousand stars
We are the mountains
And they are in us
Strangeness and beauty
Create a world we trust
Let the power be strong
And the vision be bold
Listen to the one who worships the clouds
Tales of magic, let the story be told

Robert Augustin Regnier

Never too late for courage

Holding hands on a summer night
We like the way it feels, it feels so right
My girl and I both agree
That a country fair is the place to be
April song makes for a wonderful ride
But an open book is nowhere to hide
The road is dark, a never ending line
Danger in a circle is a warning sign
So be cool I said of fire and rain
We're happy to ride on a steam train
So keep it light, breezy, and warm
Ride a powerful wind on a summer storm

A WONDERFUL DAY

I held your hand

While we strolled

We shared pictures of happy days

Let the story be bold

The rain held off

Our day is bright

I looked into your eyes

And everything is right

We are both children of God

Roses make our day

On a blanket under the sun

Our hearts are one we both can say

Robert Augustin Regnier

HOLD TIGHT

Watching the sun go down

From a back porch swing

Days are going by fast

Reminiscing is something that they bring

Country nights get a little better

When dreams end a long day

The songs we sing are like a vehicle

That hugs the road and shows the way

Free like a bird

That soars in the sky

Waiting for the first

Lover to tell us why

The things we heard

Are something to be proud of

I'm not scared of anything new

Like the warm feeling of falling in love

SERENITY STARTS NOW

You got my heart

And darn it, my soul came with it

So turn away and don't make me cry

When love came to town, it's time to quit

Just as free as we'll ever be

We sing for me and you

A whisper tells it all

So look away to a sky of blue

Dancing in the dark

Steps shine in the moon glow

Happiness will find a way

So steel away to a place we know

Robert Augustin Regnier

Go further in time

Your touch makes my pulse react
Your smile lights up the night
Poems rhyme in a spiritual way
And playing a game makes it right
I'm not sure I see
The power that goes around
I believe in the miracle
That angels would hear the sound
Tie a rope to the fever tree
Pull it tight and make it strong
Cut the tension with a knife
It's a magical balance that can't go wrong

STARS SHINE IN THE LIGHT

Two flames in a glass

Show a love that we hope will last

Sitting in our chairs

Bare feet on the ground

The flag is waving

Hear the beautiful sound

We look into each others eyes

We hold each others hand

Our love grows in colors so bright

As fireworks soar across the land

When I was young

Every hour made a new day

But now I'm older

And true love shows the way

Love in the Air

Love is in the air tonight
A touch of your hand that feels so right
Happiness is the song I sing
Love and kindness is what we bring
Try not to think of an unhappy time
Just think of tunes that rhyme
Sun over the water, fog on the bay
Sail on bye to where pirates stay
American beauty, Canadian will
Riding a wild horse is always a thrill
So it's a long hard road to cover
For God and me, sister and brother

PUT ME THROUGH

I want to fall into your arms

And give your love a try

Looking through a colored glass

That shows rain clouds in the sky

Take us on a slow ride

You and me on a beach

A window looks through time

Open a book is the lesson we teach

The lady in the black dress

Says we have nothing to lose

Lucky is the woman

Who sings the blues

I can hear echoes in the wind

And see sunshine in your eyes

Watching a rambling rose

Bloom in a world where the eagle flies

Robert Augustin Regnier

THE WHEEL AND THE SPOKE

You're my lady to see
A kiss from the deep blue sea
A whisper that touches them all
A hero in our time who stands tall
Play a song for everyone
And make it loud just for fun
Go now the path is clear
God's creative will is close and near
Do you know why we are all here?
To fight for love with nothing to fear
So pull it together up and down
The wheel and the spoke go around and around

Swifter than a horse

Swing into an island dance

Practice create and perform

Dance to a place where we stand

In the headwinds of a summer storm

Do more with pictures that tell

For they tell a lot

This is the story that finds the way

A passage of time we sometimes forgot

Three guns, three knives

We trade for a horse

Buffalo days where kindness shows

The softer side of the enemy force

And the men ran

Quickly around the camp fire

Swifter than any horse could run

Lost in a world of open desire

Robert Augustin Regnier

REMEMBER ME WHEN

Solve the puzzle

Where the black bear lays

Lazy days are mellow

Seeing through glass, colorful ways

Paint a picture

To tell a story

Winter light on the pond

Look into your heart, not to worry

There's a really good way

To climb a hill

To reach for the sky

And test your will

Red on white

The color is deep

Uncluttered is the land

Where weeping willows weep

SCENES OF ENCHANTMENT

Getting lost in this rich old world

And it feels so right

Determined to stand our ground

In the brightness of the morning light

We set out on an adventure

We ride the peace train

Follow your wishes, you have nothing to fear

Praying for the Buffalo on the open plain

Celebrate an Indian dance

Go west and conquer the heathen race

Songs around the camp fire

Send away evil without a trace

YES I AM WATCHING

Too much of nothing

Is the view from the top

More planes, more ships

Fights a battle that nobody can stop

The pendulum swings father than it should

So have a cold one and let the sun go down

Music sets the world on fire

And our senses are open to the sound

Candles on a window sill

Light them for love one by one

Grab a hold of walking away

The girl in the leather sandals strolls in the sun

Focus on the land

Ribbon of sand

Sea of blue

Wind and water

And a breeze that's true

Sea grass will grow

Unbroken in the dune

In a world of change

That shines under a yellow moon

I will go to the edge of the sea

Where healing is the flowing of time

Being more is our saving grace

In the direction of an upward climb

PAINT A PICTURE

Canvas on a railroad track

Paint a picture on the run

Be more and take more for us all

And live under the sun

Rolling thunder, prairie winds

Their voices tell us a tale

Love is the center of telling us why

Break through the fog of a wishing well

Back and forth goes the question of faith

Ideas bridge the gap of vistas clear

So paint our picture with enthusiasm and glee

And keep the creative juices near

LIVING FOR THE NIGHT

I'm living for the night
To see your eyes ever so bright
Your body has soft things to say
Told in a spiritual way
The way I feel loving you is the way
In a foggy morning of a sunny day
And I want to go crazy too
Go crazy for you
Go deep down, then reach for the sky
Pray for good times and give our love a try
Angels on my left, God on my right
Yes Joanna, I'm living for the night

Robert Augustin Regnier

THE GAMES WE PLAY

Throwing horse shoes in the sand
Sending darts in flight
Keep the spirit alive and strong
By playing games into the night
I love to hear you sing a song
I love to hear you play
On a stage where we are all at home
Friendship and kindness are here to stay
I suppose I should write it all down
The night deserves a friend
Saying "I love you" is the vision
Of brothers and sisters to the end

MILES AWAY

I had a colorful dream last night

Then I woke up at dawn

A spiritual experience sent from above

An experience that was right on

Sitting at my window gazing about

Down the valley way

It's easy to see the image seen

Of stilled voices of a sunny day

I need a vision to cling to

Simple and natural with spiritual love

I have learned the ins and outs

Of a world of beauty sent from above

PIONEERS IN SONG

The look of one or two words
The feeling for you and me
To dance and sing into the night
Sublime in nature is what we see
Question the color blue
Panic is what I'll never do
We say nothing about staying alive
A passion kiss from me to you
I will pray and find my way home
On a road where I believe caring is the way
Killing me softly is a play of dreams
Pioneers in song for tomorrow and today

My heart is sold

Girl, put your head on my shoulder

I'm sorry for making you blue

An open heart I bring

With a gift of love for you

Storm clouds gather in the sky

To make for a stormy day

Enough rain to make the crops grow

Enough for the farmers to find a way

I've seen the way I've grown

In places new and places old

I'm sitting here with a song in my head

Thank you for being my friend, my heart is sold

Robert Augustin Regnier

A LIGHT FOOTPRINT

Love only flows
When a flower grows
I reached for you but you were gone
We saw the light when you were strong
Mother to son was a two way love
The presence of art fits you like a glove
It all flows together in the songs we sing
Thinking about love is something that I bring
Bring to the dance your dreams come true
Rays of sunshine walk all over you
Some people cry and some say why not
But I say hallelujah, God's love is what we want

GONE BUT NOT FORGOTTEN

I saw an old photograph

Pictures in time

Gone but not forgotten

Are the souls on their heavenly climb

The world can't keep me down

For I'm ready for anything that it will bring

Give me the power to live this life

In harmony in love with the songs I sing

It's a drama in a play of real life

That makes the juices flow

Storytelling is what we do

To make it all happen where the spirits grow

RENAISSANCE WORLD

Sometimes I feel it slipping away

And it makes me cry

Turn and confront your shame

Where darkness rules and we wonder why

I saw good bye in your eyes

Gone is the togetherness that we knew well

A taste of honey, a sip of wine

Will rock the boat and ring the bell

Baby you don't understand

You just think about wrong

We're just minutes away

From a renaissance world that will make us strong

A TEMPEST OF FATE

The magician is real

His actions show a plan

Of dynamic change

In a world of shifting sand

Magic is played out

In a play in a dark night

It's a delicate balance of good and bad

And struggle is the winner of the good fight

I am your hero

A spirit sent from above

Fear and distress is washed away

And replaced by the welcoming hand of love

❋

COUNTRY MUSIC HEALS CABIN FEVER

A cool glass of water

Feels good on my lips

It's going to be a bright sunny day

Before the storm cloud flips

Sit up on a hill

And dream of someone to love

Tomorrow is the day

When our hearts fly with the dove

Make me a winner

Make my day

The man I see in the mirror

Will take a back road and find a way

Yes I'm having cabin fever

Let the wind blow it around

The memory of summer days come and go

And country music is a healing sound

A BORROWED SMILE

I know I hurt you

I know I let you down

A borrowed smile that I don't want to give back

That covers up a frown

A fire in the heart

Covers up the pain

Strike a match to hope and desire

And let hale fall with the rain

Sound breaks through the dark

Way down in the valley below

I'm still hurting, the heartache is real

So kiss me and our love will grow

It's just beautiful

The pictures we paint and the songs we sing

Today we are inspired

To share with our friends the love we bring

Robert Augustin Regnier

WHEN I SEE HER EYES

In the shelter of her arms

Everything seems OK

Dream of days to come

Where love will find a way

And when I see her eyes

Brightened by the sun

I'm going to think of summer days

Long days when you were the one

You and I go walking

Walking down a country lane

Say good bye to living by the gun

And look for a silver lining in clouds of rain

So that's how easy it is

The answers are here for you

It's so easy to fall in love

In a world that's spiritual and true

Two in love

Tom gave Sue a rose today

To show his love in a spiritual way

Sue gave Tom a kiss to share her love

Angels sang from high above

Flowers bloom and song birds sing

The gift of love is something that they bring

There is no higher power than what is theirs

For true love is what we all share

With God and family and you and me

The songs we sing are everything that we can be

So Tom and Sue your future is bright

Friends and family and true love will make it right

Bob Regnier

Robert Augustin Regnier

WHERE OUR SPIRITS ARE STRONG

Sometimes this world is more than I can take

It's more than I can do to walk a mile

But I forgive those who came before

The first time is the last time to smile

You're too nice and your love is true

You're the one that didn't get away

I will drive to the end of the earth

So that we can share our love another day

Warm winds blow our hearts around

Summer days are long

A country road will welcome us all

To wander where our spirits are strong

CRAWL THEN WALK

Golden nights before the end

The shadow of desire is our friend

Crawl then walk, say yes to love

Fly in colors on the wings of a dove

Experience we are, together in song

We're a chorus, a hundred strong

Take on our vision, a vision of life

Devoid of sin, hatred and strife

Take a journey, parachute into the land

Inspire to transform in shifting sand

Much of our wisdom will coexist

With tales and stories that is on our list

And the look and sound of love

Fits our world like a glove

❀ *Robert Augustin Regnier*

AN ENDLESS SONG

I want to be a superhero

Flying through the air and sky

It's all make believe I know

An endless song never saying goodbye

It never stops, this feeling inside

A feeling of love ever so strong

There's a part of me that will always be

Smiling on life, a life that's never wrong

Let's catch a rainbow

It won't be that hard to do

Writing a song and singing it slow

I go about saying I'm sorry, sometimes feeling blue

A traffic jam in the mind

Driving to a place in time

Sing it loud with love in your heart

In a place where poets make poems rhyme

GOLDEN CLOTH THEY WEAVE

All the wild animals run fast

In dreams filled with song

Live in harmony with saying goodbye

Life on the rocks, means we can't go wrong

She starts dancing when the stars come out

In a night filled with make believe

Steps in sync with a broken heart

Maidens in waiting, golden cloth they weave

The secret is out

A magic storm runs out of rain

A dark night turns into day

And people make love, looking past the pain

WRITE A PICTURE

Down by lazy brook
A stream kissed by the sun
Danny boy keeps praying
That this spiritual world will be the one
Sing a song that has no beginning
For it always was and it will always be
The message came out of thin air
With skilled hands for everyone to see
What you see is a bandwagon of hope
The splendor is real and the focus is clear
The band will arrive in grand style
And learn that salvation is near

I STILL NEED YOU

Somewhere with you

On an ocean drive

Gypsies lost in the twilight zone

On a night when music comes alive

I can hear her now

Being a little dramatic

Where song is your calling

There is no time to panic

You've never seen anyone like me

A bad boy but a sensitive man

American the beautiful all the way

Taking the long road, doing what we can

I still need you

To right the wrong

Bye bye to lonely nights

Say hello to a country song

Robert Augustin Regnier

THE FIG TREE

Fig tree grows in golden soil
Growing high into the sky
Fruit and leaves and limbs and branches
Grow ever so high

Lazy stream on falling water
Goes about its way
Harmony and togetherness
The two of them say

Take my figs for a healthy meal
All come back for more
Song and true love
Is what we have in store

Going out with my boots on

There's a story I must tell
Of a blues singer's lament
It all came together
In a quiet place where everyone was content
You're my friend, my shining star
A tower of strength, standing against a wall
But you still have to face the facts
The same golden smile shown before the fall
So tell it like it is
For the girl dances in the sun
There is so much more to do
So be part of doing it right, doing it with everyone

❊ *Robert Augustin Regnier*

Believe in me, believe in you

Reach out for me
And I'll be there for you
When times are tough
Let our love be true
Talk about her eyes so bright
They shine in the way the sun brings life
I really care about living in time
For our love is strong, you can cut it with a knife
I try to be the best man I could be
Coming on strong and following through
Exploring my inner world with grace
Living my life with God is something new

LOVE IS THE MESSAGE WE SEND

Babbling brook flowing under a bridge
Gives me serenity and opens my mind
Paint a picture to save the moment
Our experience is deliberate, expressed in kind
Can I play? The child says in a dream
The magician has something to say
Stop the world so we can hear his voice
It's fortunate that we found the way
Action is difficult but the story is bold
We are close to a devastating end
It's been painful for a very long time
But love is the message we send

Robert Augustin Regnier

A SUMMER EMBRACE

Cotton fields remember

When warm rain fell on the plain

A young girl sings

A song called champagne

Dream of a night

With countless stars and a summer breeze

A song fills the air

And a gentle wind blows through the trees

I can't wait for summer days

They will be here very soon

Welcome us all to a summer embrace

When we sing our songs under a yellow moon

ALL I WANT IS HAVING YOU

I came from afar

To a place near a tree

Leaves and branches and a solid trunk

A window in time for you and me

Watching the moon light

Shine from above

Only one wish will be granted

That of a new love

Reach for a memory

Share them in a song

I see the cottonwoods sway

In a soft wind where the days are long

I want to see the stars in your eyes

Up close where emotion comes alive

Sincerely I say it's strong

The wonders of hope ride on a one way drive

Robert Augustin Regnier

PLAY THE SOUND

A lonely boy in the middle of snow

Sings with emotion in a morning sky

Come take a peaceful view

In a storm where lonesome dreams die

I will follow the river

Through the valley, the plain, where ever it goes

Give me a shot of redemption

And finish this winter day with a rose

Play the sound

And watch it shine

Graceful are the notes

Of a soulful guitar's whine

Go tell Johnny his ship has sailed

Sail to a faraway land

Passengers on the wayward boat

Are lost in a beach of shifting sand

I'M YOUR MAN

Days go by very slow

Sometimes they seem not to go by at all

Sunshine opens up a day dream

Where characters break through before the fall

Science fiction set in the future

It's a parable in the time we live in

The magic is taken somewhere else

And when the stars shine we all win

Yesterday came suddenly

Back to where shadows covered the ground

But the birth of ideas shine for us all

And may the songs we sing go round and round

Robert Augustin Regnier

RHYME AND REASON

I know a place where we can go

Where I'm hers and she's mine

Walking to a place in time

Walking in the sunshine

Going back to country days

It's the time of the season

Her eyes were clear and bright

In the words of rhyme and reason

People around every corner

Night time shadows disappear

I loved you yesterday

It's clear you have nothing to fear

SHALL WE

Shall we dance

On a stage to a happy song

Steps that go round and round

Explore the day where we can't go wrong

Shall we sing a song

It starts my day and it feels good

Don't wait, we must do it now

Exercise with energy, I know I should

Shall we write a poem

The words will tell us so

If you are one of the many

Let the spiritual world grow

Shall we just live life

Exploring the reflective side

I walk with my shoulders back

A lifetime of learning, where fear can't hide

Robert Augustin Regnier

BLACK ON WHITE

Riding high

Till someone shouts you down

A guitar player's dream

Is haunted by the sound

Mountain country, Indian wind

Misty river where dreams come true

Go fly away tomorrow

Black on white for me and you

Guitar hero rocks and blows us away

In a show enjoyed by us all

Thank you for lifting our spirits high

Songs of power sung before the fall

Sending a Message

How can I be sure

That you are the one

Seen through rose colored glasses

Our love is certain, all said and done

Sing in a rain forest

Covered with song

How can I be sure

That love is true and the day is long

I'll be watching right or wrong

Peacemaking makes you a star

Be careful I said the change is real

Our identity is that of courage, taught from afar

�֎ *Robert Augustin Regnier*

TRUTH CALLS

A man sits on a dead stump
Just letting life go bye
Dreaming away time in a bottle
The earth's tears we sometimes cry
Call out my name
For you make me feel
That there's a warm glow inside
Stars shine brightly and our love is real
Be careful at night
For this house has ghosts in the walls
Our mission is to give and pray
Where God is a savior and truth calls

PRECIOUS LOVE

I'm weak, you're strong

The tears fell like rain

The book says stop, go back

But nothing will stop the pain

Kind hearted woman

Your story is told

Put your arms around me

Sincerely our hearts are sold

Take me back to a place I know

I hunger for your touch

Ask me how I know

That I love you so much

In time your heart will fly away

Fly on the wings of a dove

Big bad yesterday tell us more

That you belong to me, precious love

THE STORY TOLD

We all cry the same tears
When beauty gets in the way
I will read the stories told
Let the chips fall where they may
Sing a song and reach for tomorrow
Fight for love all over this land
I'm in love with hearts that care
Never putting our heads in the sand
What does it take for us to see
When music will conquer and overcome
It's about living life together with you
The fight for love is enough for some

Sophisticated dance

Mellow by the music

Stand by your man

Shed a little light

Taking it as fast as we can

So we walk on the earth

And I am the one

That sees our vision clearly

Going forward, always having fun

You're a romantic

A dreamer like me

Imagine there's no words to rhyme

Heaven is where I want to be

Join me in showing the world

Protecting it from our worst fears

Paradise lost in many ways

Stand by your love fighting back tears

❀ *Robert Augustin Regnier*

A ROAD THAT'S LONG

Her hair was jet black

It framed her eyes in a color so bright

Meet me where lovers cry

Tears in shadows of a dark night

The pulse is strong

And the vision is clear

Hear the whisper of a summer breeze

Our love is alive with serenity near

Don't wait for victory

Just listen to the song

Played in the dark side of goodbye

The journey we travel is on a road that's long

TICK TOCK

A clock that doesn't work

Tells the time twice a day

A love that reaches further

Only the best will give sway

Try not to think of what went wrong

For we can make up our own rules

There's space at the inn with room to spare

And the gift of love is a treasure full of jewels

You make me see clearly

All the way to the end of time

Clouds and storms were nowhere in sight

And the search for love goes on an upward climb

✿ *Robert Augustin Regnier*

Magical World

Don't try to tell me

About living someone else's dreams

Mine are true borrowed in time

The fire that burns is not what it seems

I hope she doesn't forget me

When days are long and skies are blue

I count my blessings one by one

Ready for love, a solitary life that's true

Capture an image

The story is told

Enter the world of make believe

Wake up the past the program is sold

Be still be still let us change who we are

Beauty happens when we fight for love

Fascination doesn't slow us down

But a magical world will come from above

Compare to real

Ships with painted sails

Sail into the night

With treasure days on their minds

Sailors dream of futures bright

Fight for glory

Rhythm of the past

The battle goes forward

With a focus that will last

I am ready

Sixty seconds to count down

I know it will be OK

If we fall, we will fall from the sound

Life at the top

Moving at the speed of light

Fall on your sword

Let the story be bright

JOHNNY LEGEND

Home is where the sun shines

Peaceful warriors quiet their guns

Let it speak to the passion of art

Very close to a river that runs

My work is full of questions

Creativity is bold, sometimes crying out

Go back to the days of make believe

When our world lets our winners shout

Half the time we dance

The other half we make love

It's hard to balance our spiritual life

Large is our celebration sent from above

HAVE A NIGHT THAT YOU'LL NEVER FORGET

No more sorrow

No more pain

Up against an open door

Let the small be said in vain

I hope it will last for years to come

This show that was written for us in mind

I'm waiting for you to stand tall

The mission we seek is the mission we find

Is your heart filled with pain

Let us sing and in the spring we pray

That we will hear church bells ring

And sing our songs in the morning of a sunny day

Robert Augustin Regnier

SHADOW OF A LIVING MIND

The knock of a stick is not lost

On a dress the color of white

How are we going to spend the time

We honor the things we do that's right

Deeds of loving kindness

Elevate the soul

If you can see me clearly

The sights, the sounds, the feelings is our goal

God will be present

I read the wise man's book

The culture is our salvation

And the white light is the gift we took

I want to die in my sleep

The ghosts will leave the spirit behind

A lifelong quest for a spiritual home

Is lost in the shadow of a loving mind

An extra set of eyes

The song is the silence

Finding words and melody

Memories never lose their pleasure

The standard is set for you and me

Sunshine washes away

Sin from the other side of the street

We did everything right

In the theater where we all meet

Across the street

Across the ocean

Love brings us together

And puts our hearts in motion

Deep in the valley

On top of the hill

A loving heart is where it belongs

And an extra set of eyes is always a thrill

Robert Augustin Regnier

A DARK DAY

You live with the wind

And die with it slowing down

You run in step with saying goodbye

A fools game too big to be around

A fiddle plays a sentimental tune

In a midday storm that looked like night

Come quick, come high the black blizzard rages

I'm beginning to see that the end is in sight

Drifting clouds of dust

Blowing across the plain

Hope keeps us going

Until God sends us rain

She called to me

In a song sent from above

A quiet day seemed to be our lot

A pretty day filled with love

I FOUND THE WORDS

Put your faith in the wind

Silver bullet becomes a fire

Be proud and take it back

For hope sometimes finds the desire

She takes me downtown

Where she works her magic

One day equals many more

A place where hope defies logic

To hear somebody say

You don't know me

To see the proud come around

And climb the fever tree

She's the song I play

A melody sung for all

It will not take more than a memory

To rock me like the wind before the fall

THE YEAR BEFORE

I come to it with love

A shift of power with a lot of work to do

There's a saying that says "do it right"

Our responsibility is to protect the color blue

Yes you've won the lottery of life

Great people join me along the way

A drop in the bucket, a wave in the ocean

Unbroken in our resolve for tomorrow and today

Kill the calf, the children must eat

A grade school education with many mouths to fed

The mist and the rain have much to say

Many prayers were said that showed us the way

SPIN AND WEAVE

Yes I surrender

To the morning light

It's all in the words we say

And not much time to do it right

What did the soul survivor want

What did his partner demand

I always stood tall

In a garden of roses where I made my stand

The sun keeps setting

Day after lonely day

Swing at the first pitch

In a game we all play

Imagine a country road

Crossing a railroad track

When you say my name

Our minds come together and we can never go back

THE CHEETAH

I take a step

Pause

It's out there

Three steps, I pause again

I think I can get him

I start my run

I'm at full stride

I'm gaining on him

He's fast but I'm faster

He turns to the left

I'm right behind

I catch him but he gets away

I chase him but he's gone

Oh well there will be next time

A THOUSAND MILES DOWN

Show me the way

To a long slow song

The path we follow

Is a path that's long

The guitar player calls it a day

And finds happiness in quiet times

He strums and picks his song so bright

And makes our melodies dance and rhyme

A thousand miles down

Then a left turn

No bigger than an eyelash

Is the lesson we learn

Back at the ranch

The story is told

Rewrite the book

Let the words be bold

HAVE YOU EVER SEEN SKIES SO BLUE

There is no one but us
To weather the storm
And find our way home
When days are warm
So I'm coming after you
Coming after your love
I love your blue eyes and dark hair
And all the grace sent from above
The river flows between the hills
The eagle nests in an oak tree
The powerful ride on a strong wind
And a rock is solid and everything that we can be

Ride the storm

Somewhere with you

Somewhere with me

Meet me in the middle

Where our eyes will see

Our lives from the inside out

The soul in the body of everyone

July comes and goes in a rush

Trust your heart with love under the sun

Where do they go

They come here

To fight for tomorrow

And wash away a tear

Paint it red

The color of the way I feel

Memories help me play a song

Memories made of iron and steel

THE GOOD STUFF

The good stuff
It's all we need
Playing a song grooving along
With friends in the lead
We'll never get away
With tear drops to hide
Radio blasts your soul down tight
Gives your memory a free ride
This is where the good times shine
Sing like a bird and make me smile
If you want a little bit of everything
Find your vision and walk a mile

SEE THE SUN

Sara goes wishing

Wishing she had nice clothes

She struggles to see

The highs from the lows

Wish on a star

Wish that I may be

A ticking clock that hears my voice

A sad song played for you and me

Dive in deep water

Her story has not a single lie

Find the solution to all our woes

Our message to you is say good bye

Watch the planets in the night

See the sun rise and fall

The artist slips away

And makes the final call

SAY HELLO, MY SPECIAL FRIEND

Every time you close your eyes

A warm wind finds its way

Every time we sing a song

Harmony will give sway

The band is all fired up

Sailing ribbons in the air

The world is our stage

With all the weight there is to bare

Shapes and numbers against a wall

There's no sound to help us along

A ball, a cube, a circle in space

Our lesson to you is quiet and strong

So a puppet flashes his mighty sword

A young girl throws a kiss

Victory is coming soon

And saying I love you is something we'll never miss

DANGEROUS WORLD

There is talk on the street

It says love is here

Hey pretty girl, what do you think

She thinks truth has nothing to fear

The world keeps spinning fast

It might be time to get off

Rediscover the games we play

We land in a place that welcoming and soft

Because you believe

In a world of beauty and grace

Try not to fall in a trap of fear

Dangerous world, gone without a trace

THE VOICE OF WHAT'S HAPPENING

Between two fires

The battle goes on

A warrior fights as a free man

And a spy for all seasons to gaze upon

The search for glory

Has a noble ending

Rough is the answer

The challenge has our fences mending

A woman in battle

Fights like a man

It has to be fictional

A romance set upon the land

Watch our night turn into day

And give a little bit of love

Victory is the goal

That fits us like a glove

A JOURNEY IN TIME

I heard a song

It sent me to another place

Music is a confidence builder

Played in a world of satin and lace

I read a book

Reach for life and the stage is set

For romance tells a compelling tale

Where all the sacraments of love are met

I saw a film

The light shined in

Comfortable is our modern world

Frowned upon is mortal sin

It has to do with the journey of the soul

Three days to say goodbye

Straighten up and call a friend

It takes talent and never asking why

✳

TRAVEL TO THE REVOLUTION

Don't wake me up

I might come alive

The beautiful expression of nature

Express the commitment in time to survive

The artist captures the moment

And looks to the past

Visions of color turns to magic

Singers of beauty make the image last

Tear it down history begs

Take me down to the highway of tomorrow

Dance and strut with golden legs

Make our way in heartache and sorrow

Sing in our home together in song

A song in harmony for all of us

"What will it look like" Sally says

A world of beauty that always was

HUMMINGBIRD

Beautiful hummingbird fly along

Kiss a flower like a song

Underneath an Amarillo sky

Never letting our dreams run dry

Hard to spot

Easy to miss

Nectar of the Gods

Summertime kiss

Flowers bloom where hummingbirds live

Love and peace is something that they give

Hummingbirds say "This is our town"

We fly around and around and around

Robert Augustin Regnier

THE FINAL SONG

Pretty faces and diamond rings
Say hello to happy things
Lilacs are gone for another day
It will be a year before they come our way
Time goes by, days pass
Beautiful pictures the story will last
Work and toil the hours away
Then play a game have fun today
It all goes by the gifted and the strong
Sunshine sings the final song

SILVER AND GOLD

Lost in a deep love that is here

Brings us back around

Sing a melody, capture the voice

Hold out your hand let us share the sound

My heart is sad and lonely

Let us pretend then turn away

When we're in the moment

Love will come another day

Yes I think it's going to work

Turn a page, a story is told

Speak low, love is a spark

Find a voice in silver and gold

NOTHING'S SLOWING US DOWN

Passing days go by so slow

When the sun reaches the sky

Loneliness comes in an easy way

Like a clown showing us why

It's important to me to write the words

Letters talk and come alive

Let the little girl dance and sing

Simple is the need to survive

I saw the actress shed a tear

Then a smile came to her face

At the end of the day time stood still

And the musician says thank you with style and grace

CREEP ALONG THE ROAD

I can't take another heartache

It has given me silver hair

Silver hair doesn't press

The limits that we all share

Good bye to sorrow

Our never ending bond

Peace and joy sent into this world

Is a gift from a magic wand

Mystifying mister rules the world

But the boys in the band has had enough

We live for your mercy

And after a thousand miles the road gets rough

One simple key

Unlocks the door

A few words to say

Means love ever more

INNOCENT OF BLUE FIRE

The night is quiet

The lion has bedded down

So rest your little hand on mine

Still is the sound

I'll go anywhere with you

Forever ever we'll never part

Shadows will fall all over town

Loving you will always be smart

How long have I waited

Waited for your love

Don't let me be the last to know

Let the warm wind blow turtle dove

ROLLING THUNDER

The feel of misty air
In a quiet forest of green
Iron horse rolls by a river
And the most beautiful hills ever seen
Rolling thunder
Claps of sound
Frighten the livestock
Danger to be around
Strolling through town
Hat in my hand
Breathtaking views
Seen across the land
Savage winters
Are a thing of the past
Stampeders tell
A story that will last

COLOR MY WORLD

It's been a long time

Since I colored in a book

The color of memories

Take a lifelong look

Color the morning

In shades of blue

Red and green

And purple too

Many colors

High and low

Brings us joy

At the end of a rainbow

We have so much

In common with paint

Color me joyful

In the arms of a saint

Do you believe?

Yes I do

That my favorite color

Is the color blue

LOVE SPOON

I painted a picture on my spoon

The picture of love, the face of a cartoon

Eyes of fire, hair of blue

Painted in colors for me and you

Will my spoon ever see the soup

Heating the stove completes the loop

Country spoon, weather spoon

Summer spoon, amazing spoon

All in one lives in my drawer

Love is the picture on my spoon

To be seen evermore

Robert Augustin Regnier

AN UNDERSTANDING WAY

Whistle blows a warning sound
Danger from broken glass
Take me back to a story told
Fire and water, this too will pass
Where else do hero's walk
Walk where music fills the air
Scarlet ribbons, the guitar player plays
Whistling tunes in a place where
Songs live to be sung with grace
Patsy makes it easy and true
Say the things you used to say
Love songs for me and you

A MORNING KISS

A morning kiss on a summer day

Days in the sun when you were the one

Each night before you go to bed

Dream in colors under the sun

Big girls don't cry

But they weep tears of joy

Thunder and lighting is something good

And a hush for a girl and a boy

Keep it alive and kicking

Too many tear drops on the floor

Remember when you held my hand

Memories of love evermore

❋ *Robert Augustin Regnier*

WAGON WHEEL

Heaven help the one who did her wrong

From here to there the answer is in a song

Lazy day brings mist that cries

Rain hides the tears in my eyes

A night like this runs out of moonlight

But the skies are clear, stars shining bright

The soul of a woman is proud and strong

Easy to love down a road that's long

You never know what stormy weather will bring

Thunder and lighting and a song to sing

So please don't take it wrong

For love will come in a song

TIME OF THE SEASON

Suzanne holds the mirror

That reflects love evermore

Time in a bottle, sands of time

Many years of singing is what we have in store

Yes I like the sound

Bring me back to a living dance

Hallelujah the band is well

And lost in a dream of never ending romance

The man in a hat sings a song

The melody is before your eyes

The crowd picks up the beat

And the camera tells no lies

The message is to you is

Please don't get in the way

The fight for art and action

Is a battle for another day

Robert Augustin Regnier

DANCE IS A STYLE

Give me the heart

Give me the soul

Give me more

And make it whole

Let the children dance

Let them dance and sing

On a stage of yellow and green

A place where solitude is something we bring

We try to achieve many good things

But evil waits at every turn

Wonderful is our guiding light

Who better to love is the lesson we learn

So on the first day

The dance will go on

Love me gently

A girl sings a song

LOVE KNOCKING ON MY DOOR

Kiss me again

Kiss me like that

Leaves in the air

Loving you is where it is at

Sun in your hair

This summer with you

It matters to me

That our love is true blue

So go now

And join in a song

Cruise to a place that's near

A place where our love is strong

❋ *Robert Augustin Regnier*

THE SPIRIT GROWS

Hey girl, keep your heart wide open
When cruising down a back road
Shadows at night tell a story
And the girl in blue cracks the code
Let the wind blows us around
The storm is all we can handle
A trip down memory lane
Guided by the glow of a candle
So looking back at life
Nothing perfect, God tells us so
The poet makes our world come alive
And lets our spirit thrive and grow

SLEEP TIGHT

It's two in the morning

Dreams are starting to unfold

Eyes are closing

And the story of the day has been told

Free as a bird

The night sails on

Thank God we have

This pillow to dream upon

So two o'clock is late

But not for us

The night goes on bye

And go to sleep we must

Robert Augustin Regnier

Moving and making in

Put a candle in the window

Light it for peace and story telling

We'll keep our faith alive and well

A story told where tears are welling

Yes we don't have to cry

Because we're knocking at the door

Unforgettable and looking good

The things we did right are giving us more

Are you sincere?

Are you strong?

It's a great way to live

This world in a song

Back in time again

Here I am living with my hurt

Trying to be real and true

I'm no longer stuck in time

Groups of broken people pray for me and you

So keep away from heartache

Let the healing start

We're all God's children

Loving together so let us not part

So let's have a spot of tea

And dream of a pathway for our love

With open arms we will survive

The magic touch of a golden glove

❋ *Robert Augustin Regnier*

I CAN HEAR YOUR VOICE

Say my name

Clearly in the night

It sounds so good when you say it

In harmony with birds in flight

Say my name

So everyone can hear

The beauty of your voice

Sung in colors so soft and clear

So when you say my name

I'll be waiting for sparks to fly

Making love till the sun comes up

A focus in time where lovers never cry

About the Author

He has an easy way about him. Born in the 40's, growing up in the 50's, coming of age in the 60's. This gave him a foundation of values and vision that has seen good things happen for him, his family and all who share in his work. Being positive is the catch word that encompasses his poetry. Subjects of love, spirituality, and good feelings is something he tries to bring to all of his friends. He has made his living as a craftsman, carpenter by trade. And through the years this has given him a wealth of rewarding experiences, lasting personal relationships, and many interesting stories shared among those he encountered. So Bobby wants you to sit back in your chair, couch, or hammock for a moment and just get lost in his world of beauty that he has written for all.